C000157269

The user's guide to the Rabbit

The user's guide to the Rabbit

Marcelle Perks

Careful now

Sex toys have been designed to give you more fun, so make sure you get the best out of them by being picky about the material they are made from and ensuring any lubricant you use is compatible. Good maintenance ensures your love tools are always ready to hand; store your vibes separately to the batteries and clean according to the manufacturer's instructions or as is appropriate to the material that your toy is made from. Don't be too zealous with using toys, it's best to go slow at first and use plenty of lube to speed things along!

Although the websites mentioned were checked at the time of going to press, the World Wide Web is constantly changing. This means that the publisher and author cannot guarantee the contents of any websites mentioned in the text.

Copyright © The Infinite Ideas Company Limited, 2006

The right of Marcelle Perks to be identified as the author of this book has been asserted in accordance with the Copyright, Designs and Patents Act 1988.

First published in 2006 by
The Infinite Ideas Company Limited
36 St Giles, Oxford, OX1 3LD, United Kingdom
www.infideas.com

A CIP catalogue record for this book is available from the British Library
ISBN 10: 1–904902–80–4
ISBN 13: 978–1–904902–80–5
Brand and product names are trademarks or registered trademarks of their respective owners.
Designed and typeset by Baseline Arts Ltd, Oxford
Printed by Acorn Press, Swindon, UK

Contents

Introduction

It's astonishing what kind of reaction you get when you tell people you're writing a book about Rabbit vibrators! People assume everybody knows how to use one, but in reality there's very little information available. Although these products sell in their millions, the industry is largely privately owned and there is no watchdog or consumer scheme to cover such personal devices. Typically sex toys contain no product literature; sex educator Cory Silverberg says, "Unlike almost any other consumer product area, because it's sex nobody wants to talk about it."

For this book, I gathered key information by going directly to sex toy manufacturers and people who sell sex products to consumers. I also interviewed international sexologists and therapists, sex and research experts, together with some enthusiastic Rabbit users who were happy to share some of their practical tips. Thanks to the generosity of my

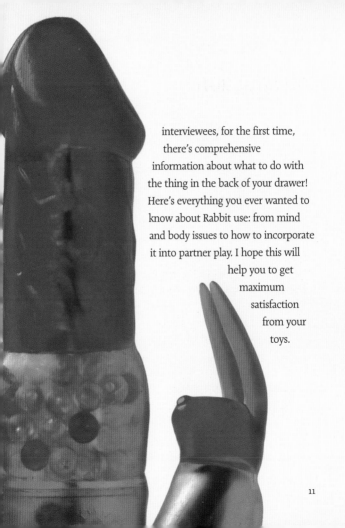

interviewees, for the first time, there's comprehensive information about what to do with the thing in the back of your drawer! Here's everything you ever wanted to know about Rabbit use: from mind and body issues to how to incorporate it into partner play. I hope this will help you to get maximum satisfaction from your toys.

1

Why use a sex toy?

A Rabbit doesn't just have to be for masturbation.

Around half the women in the UK own a sex toy and the best selling model worldwide is the Rabbit, a dual-action vibe designed to titillate both clitoral and vaginal areas. Online retailer LoveHoney.co.uk sells 1000 every month and even Princess Anne's daughter Zara Phillips has hosted an Ann Summers party.

A vibrator works by producing an intense oscillating rhythm that is faster than any human hand, and the Rabbit's bunny ears are designed to stimulate the clitoris – the area where most women experience satisfying orgasms. Vibrators aren't just used for masturbation by single women; research shows that people who use sex aids have sex more frequently and experience more satisfying sex with a partner. Here you will find lots of tips for things to do with a partner and also an explanation of how to use your Rabbit in detail, because many women are simply too embarrassed to ask everything they need to know.

A Rabbit triggers more nerve endings than a penis, and people who like Rabbits like them *a lot*. Geri Halliwell says that when a friend gave her a vibrator it was 'life-changing'. Ann Summers' vibe expert, Gita Selli, explains why they're so popular: 'Rabbits give something called a blended orgasm where the woman has two orgasms in one go – she's having an external *and* an internal orgasm.' Using a vibe is also safe sex, and a vibe never says no. What are you waiting for?

2

Medical benefits

Did you know that vibrator use has positive health benefits and is even recommended for some treatments?

From its very beginnings, vibrator use has been linked to medical benefits. The first prototypes in the 1880s were cranky electromechanical devices used by doctors to relieve women of 'hysteria'. Although we know vibrators are beneficial, there's no fantastic data to back this up because there has been no large-scale clinical trial to date. Because most sex toys are sold as 'novelties' rather than as medical products manufacturers don't conduct clinical trials, as to do so would change their classification and make them more expensive to produce.

The 2004 Berman study, 'The Health Benefits of Sexual Aids and Devices', found nearly half of women aged 18 to 55 had used a vibrator and that women who use them have more interest in sex, reach orgasm more easily and are more likely to have a better quality of life. This may be the tip of the iceberg, sex educator Cory Silverberg says: 'There are so few legitimate studies of sex toy use that we actually have no idea how many people use these toys, although sales alone suggest it is a substantial number. Sex toys do get used in clinical studies on sexual arousal; however, this isn't mentioned – the focus is not on the vibrator but on the response.'

Although we know that vibrators do improve sexual health and well-being, there's precious little data to reassure consumers. You'll just have to try it and see!

3

The ABC of vibes

Choosing the best vibrator material and shape for your needs.

Before you buy a vibrator it helps if you're familiar with what gets you off best whilst masturbating. If you enjoy a lot of clitoral stimulation, pay close attention to the shape and vibe potential of the bunny ears. For women who love their G-spot being probed, the shape, angle and distance between the clitoral stimulator relative to the shaft are crucial measurements. Women who are extra sensitive just inside their vagina will want models that provide stronger pearl-action friction. If you like to be tickled around the anal area at the same time, then there are models that pleasure all three zones at once.

If you already have a vibe, you'll have more of an idea of what shape and size suits you. The different materials Rabbits are made from give a different feel: there's latex, silicone, jelly, metal and PVC. PVC, jelly and silicone are good at conducting vibrations, but jelly toys are more porous and harder to clean and can contain potentially harmful chemicals called phthalates. Silicone is easier to clean and medical grade silicone is hypoallergenic, but some women prefer the gentler, more realistic feel provided by softer materials.

Noise is an important factor if you don't want everyone to know what you are up to! The most important consideration is the frequency of the various vibes, so you need to go to a sex shop and test out the models on offer.

4

Getting technical

The ins and outs of selecting
a toy.

Many people prefer to buy their vibes from sex shops. It's
really essential to be able to see, touch, feel and smell any toy
you want to buy. If you are buying something for use with
your partner, then you should *both* go. Gita Selli, Ann
Summers' vibe expert says, 'I normally tell couples to come
in together because then the woman can actually look at the
toys and decide whether she feels comfortable with it.' Men
invariably assume the best vibe is the longest and the
thickest phallic-shaped object they can find, but for most
women the clit action is the real deal. Don't get too
distracted by the frenetic movement of the pearl beads in
the Rabbit model's shaft; you'll feel more on the clitoral area,
so pay particular attention to the bunny ears.

SMOKING ACCESSORIES

*VIBRATORS*PUMPS*

OBACCO ACCESSORIES

*LOTIONS*GELS*

GAGS*SEX TOYS*

BLOW-UP DOLLS*

*VIDEOS*DVD*

LINGERIE

BOOKS*GIFTS

LUBES

Choose a female-friendly specialist store that is well-lit and has properly trained staff to test out vibes. Ask if you can test out a model that you like the look of with some batteries. Rather than testing it on your nose, Gita Selli says, 'I normally tell customers to put it on their hip bone just on the inside or on the muscle between the shoulder blade and the spine, because those are areas that will relax the customer.' To feel both vibe actions, cup your hand and place the bunny ears on the fleshy skin between your finger and thumb whilst your hand grips the shaft.

5

Getting in the mood

Before you get down to it manually, here's how to psych yourself up for love play.

Sex therapists recommend vibrators a lot. They're good for providing physical stimulation where sometimes people can't provide it. However, although a Rabbit can mechanically stimulate you, often you need to be mentally aroused first in order to feel the full effects.

To encourage women to feel sexy, Relate sex therapist Jane Roy says, 'We make suggestions that are very much tailored to the individual – it might be something simple like getting erotic literature to read or finding a video to watch. I would discuss with them what sort of material and what fantasy figures make them feel sexy. They can also fantasise about good times in the past with their partner.'

It's often subtle things that can get you going – like a favourite romantic comedy or an old song that brings back memories. For some women, chilling out in a hot bath and painting their nails helps to relax them. You might want to use a bit of private space for fantasy or actively seek out sexy images or stories on the internet.

Another tip is to get into aural pleasure – sexy audio stories that you can listen to as you prepare yourself. Jill-Evelyn Hellwig from the Fun Factory also suggests you call your partner to talk dirty if you're on your own. The sexiest organ is really the brain, so do what needs to be done to get mentally turned on.

6

Smoochy tickles

Tickle your mouth with your Rabbit and make your lips tingle.

Our lips are underrated as an erogenous zone, but think about how longingly you've kissed people in the past and you'll realise they make an ideal starting point for vibe play. Ensure your Rabbit is clean and play with the controls until you get the bunny ears buzzing.

The best way to hold the Rabbit for this is with the control panel in your hand, and with the penis-like shaft end pointing downwards towards your breasts. Slowly trace lines just with the buzzing bunny ears on the outlines of your lips. The nerve networks are more densely packed towards your lip line and you'll probably be surprised at their reaction when blood starts pumping to the area you've just primed. After a minute or so, take the bunny away and pucker your lips up to savour the sensation. It leaves them throbbing!

Have regular little intervals to give your lips a break, but there's endless fun to have with your new throbbing friend. You can dip the ears inside your mouth for a different effect and run the ears around and inside the lip line, try circles and figures of eight, and practise working your vibe in deft, tantalising movements that later you'll be able to use elsewhere!

If you're with a partner, you can also kiss and experiment with bunny lip action on each other. For an added treat try it with something you can smear on your lips, like Kamasutra's lip balm.

7

What if I don't like to masturbate?

Women who masturbate are more likely to have more and better orgasms with someone else. But what if the idea of it turns you off?

Sex researcher Dr Petra Boynton says, 'We know women who don't want to touch their vagina with their fingers who might find a sex toy useful, although the reasons underlying their dislike of touching their bodies should be explored with a psychosexual therapist.' Although some researchers worry that sex toys have been over-hyped by series like *Sex and the City*, sexologist Yvonne K Fulbright points out, 'One of the good things is that it has been permission-giving, it's advertised the Rabbit, normalising it and making it acceptable to use.' If you don't like to touch yourself with your fingers, you'll find the Rabbit more user-friendly, and you don't *have* to use it on your genitals.

Counsellors like Relate sex therapist Jane Roy don't insist their clients learn to masturbate: 'Women are either already masturbating or they're not. And if not, it's often because they feel that you shouldn't touch yourself. So those inhibitions need to be talked through before a woman feels comfortable masturbating. Some of the women in therapy are content with their sex lives with their partner, but are still not comfortable about masturbation.'

If you feel masturbation is not for you, get your partner to use vibe play on you. Use a helping hand with the power controls and just enjoy.

8

Body melt

Not many people realise that
you can also use your handy
vibrator to give an all-over
relaxing massage.

It's best to begin using a sex toy by rubbing it over parts of
your body like your face, neck and stomach to experiment
with the speed. You might prefer a lighter stroking action, or
firm pressure. Also experiment with massage oils and
lubricants (and feel free to try a genital lubricant elsewhere for
a change). Some women like to caress themselves through
their silk underwear.

Sex educator Cory Silverberg thinks people underestimate
the pleasure of using vibes non-sexually: 'To me that's the

nice thing about a product like the Hitachi magic wand which was designed for full body massage, and you can use it for that, but you might discover it also feels good between your legs. However, genital stimulation is just one part of making you feel good.'

Underrated areas of the body, like the neck, are very sensitive. Use the bunny ears to target specific spots and get the shaft part gyrating on larger, fleshy areas. Every person has a unique sexual response, so don't be surprised if you enjoy stimulation in an unexpected area. Saleswoman Juli-Ann Ledger found she enjoyed using her vibe on her feet: 'I really love having my feet tickled. My Platinum Rabbit has got little speed settings and I used the bunny ears to massage my feet and found it really good.' Don't worry about feeling horny, just relax.

9

Nipple ripples

The stimulating bunny can also be used on other erogenous zones — like your nipples.

Nipples are also sex organs and respond well to vibe action – some women can even orgasm from nipple stimulation! The problem is they're normally a cursory part of foreplay and tend to get ignored as the action moves to second base. If you're with a partner, drizzle lube over your nipples and get him/her to fondle them as they would a clitoris. Don't let your partner stop there though; your breasts should be explored all over. For some it's the fold of skin underneath that gets them going: saleswoman Juli-Ann Ledger says, 'My nipples don't seem to be massively sexual, it's more effective getting the shaft's stimulator going underneath the boobs. It's really relaxing and tingles, and if your partner is doing it, it's getting into foreplay.'

Tease the outside of your breasts first. Once you get to the nipples, get your partner to trace lines around your areolae, and they can also stroke the nipple with the same movement they use on your clit. For advanced play, sexpert Emily Dubberley suggests, 'Something that can be quite nice is effectively a tit wank with a vibrator, because depending on what size your breasts are you can get dual nipple stimulation. Set the vibrator going and get your partner to slide it between your breasts while you hold your nipples together near the vibes.' Wow! There are also nipple creams and nipple clamps you can play with to get you over the edge.

10

Clitoral joy

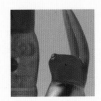

If you're not ready to tackle the Rabbit all in one go, try the junior size models — like the Mini Rabbit — to enjoy clitoral stimulation.

Although the traditional sex toy has been penis-shaped, in reality women respond best to clitoral stimulation, which is why the Rabbit is useful in offering dual stimulation at once. It could be that you need to focus first purely on your clitoral area, and there are mini Bunnys or clitoral stimulators you can use to tease yourself.

Danish sexologist Helle Koldsø recommends that women spend time teasing themselves with a vibe externally first: 'There is so much more to it than just that one small spot and I like to discover how sensitive the areas around my clitoris are. If I go exactly to the spot, I'm finished nearly before I've begun. If I start more slowly around the area, and stop and remove the sex toy every time I feel an orgasm is coming closer and start again, the orgasm, when I finally allow it to come, is so much stronger.'

Try liberally using lots of lube to help things along. You can also experiment to find out what speed and rhythm turns you on most and which type of stroke works best for you. For some women, it's as precise as the left side of the clitoris being more sensitive than the right. Some clitoral stimulators are just for external use only, but others can be 'dipped in' as well.

"Good sex is like
good bridge.
If you don't have
a good partner,
you'd better have
a good hand."

Mae West

11

Below the belt

If you're still not quite warmed up, use the bunny ears to massage your perineum before heading for where X marks the spot.

When you are first testing out the bunny ears on your clitoris, the shaft of the vibrator will be bumping against your bum cheeks. You might find this pleasurable – and you can experiment with turning on the gyrating shaft to see if the rocking sensation touches a nerve. If the lips of your labia are more sensitive (they are in about 10% of women), you could also try the bunny ears and/or the tip of the gyrating shaft and slowly glide down to the perineum (the jut of skin between your vagina and anus). A trickle of lube will help things along, but remember you can't use the same bit of your vibe on both vagina and perineum. If you want the fun without the fuss, leave your pants on and let the vibe tickle you through the material. If it feels really good, you can turn the Rabbit around so that the bunny ears are directly doing perineum-pleasing work.

If you find this area stimulating, think about trying specially designed Rabbits like the Double Bunny Rabbit Vibrator, which has an extra bunny ear to tickle your nether regions. You can also buy a purpose-built anal vibrator or butt plug to use in conjunction with clitoral and vaginal stimulation from your Rabbit. Talk about being spoiled for choice!

12

First time

Here's how to gradually introduce genital play.

Ideally you should experiment with all sorts of toys to figure out what works best for you. Icelandic sexologist Yvonne K Fulbright says, 'For a beginner vibrator I would suggest something less intimidating and less complicated than a Rabbit. That's for women who need stronger, more varied stimulation, or who have already experimented with their hands, partner or a less complicated vibrator.'

Cory Silverberg, co-owner of the Toronto-based sex shop Come As You Are, says, 'We're a lot of people's first-time sex store experience. When people come in for the first time we often suggest something that would be good both for penetration and clitoral stimulation because often they don't know what they like. We would recommend a toy that would allow you to explore your whole body – something like the Pocket Rocket that allows you to find out where you like stimulation best.'

Make sure you are aroused first and use plenty of lube. Pay attention to your clitoris and insert the vibrator turned off, to get used to its feel. Gita Selli, Ann Summers' vibe expert, has this advice for first-time Rabbit users: 'Use the bunny stimulator just on the clitoris first, play around on the labia and the nerve endings with the little bunny rabbit using lots of lubrication. Slowly just twist in the shaft rather than pushing it in, which causes less friction.'

Don't rush things or expect to hit the jackpot the first few times you experiment.

13

Down and dirty

Tip-top cleaning and maintenance tips to make light work of cleaning up.

No matter how drunk or tired I am, I never go to bed without taking off my make-up. In the same way, get into a routine where you clean sex toys after use. Depending on your Rabbit's material, there are different procedures, so always ask at the store how to care for your toy. Unless your vibe is waterproof, hold it so that the casing containing the batteries doesn't get immersed or splashed with water.

Most Rabbits are primarily PVC, a porous material, so it is best to use a specially designed wipe, such as Buzz Fresh, to clean your toys. Don't use baby wipes, as they contain oil

which damages PVC and silicone. The Fun Factory's Jill-Evelyn Hellwig says, 'For silicone, all you have to use is mild soap and water. If you feel you need to disinfect the toy, we tell our clients to be cautious because if you use any disinfectant it can damage the mucous membranes of the vagina.' Latex and cyberskin materials are more porous and vulnerable, so use only mild soap or a specially designed cleaner for these.

Don't throw or drop sex toys and if you take the batteries out after use, you'll get more use out of both. Take pride in your toy collection and keep them handy, you never know when you might use them!

14

The clitoral rub

You can use the shaft of the vibrator as well as the specially designed Rabbit ears to give your clitoris a buzz.

If you've experimented with a mini vibe or the gentle application of your Rabbit's bunny ears and know you can tolerate the buzz, you're ready for more action. Pay lots of attention to your clitoris: even women like Rabbit-user Nicole Smith, who enjoys the dual features of her Rabbit, admits, 'It's more about clitoral stimulation for me.'

If your Rabbit vibrator has the traditional bunny ears, then you can experiment with putting one on each side of your clitoris and turning on the power. You might find that one side is more sensitive than the other or that you prefer a clockwise or anti-clockwise motion. Try using a mirror to look and see what's happening – you should be able to see your clitoris enlarging and getting redder as you get turned on. Move and adjust the bunny ears accordingly. You can also switch on the gyrating shaft externally and see how this feels whirling against your clitoris. Experiment with as many different vibe speeds and movements as you can.

Some Rabbits have a rounded nub rather than ears, which concentrates the vibrations into a smaller area. I saw a stripped down Twist & Shake model at the Fun Factory and observed how much stronger the clitoral vibe was. Experiment and test out all the possibilities of your Rabbit to get the full effects.

15

Softening the sex-fx

If the vibrations are too
intense for you, here's how to
soften the vibe until you're
ready for it.

When using a Rabbit on yourself or someone else, one of the
trickiest things is getting the right tempo of throbbing vibe.
Many women try to force-feed their clitoris into overdrive,
but if you over-stimulate this sensitive area then, basically,
you go numb. Every clitoris varies in sensitivity depending on
anatomical shape and the positioning of the nerve endings.
Even if you know where touch feels good, explore a wider
area – the clitoris has 'arms' under the skin that can extend
as far back as nine centimetres, and some women have more

nerve endings in their labia. The golden rule is to start slow and explore your sensitivities.

You may experience oversensitivity. Sex educator Cory Silverberg points out, 'As a result of some disabilities and medications, some people experience hypersensitivity. For those people a vibrator would be horrible.' Ask your doctor if you're not sure.

If you have problems dealing initially with over-stimulation, use some form of barrier to soften the sex-fx. Danish sexologist Helle Koldsø says, 'Some women talk about that problem. You can soften it by putting something between the skin and the sex toy like keeping your pants on, or using the sheet or even vibrating through a couple of fingers to soften it.' Remember sex is a personal response: Koldsø explains, 'For me it's the opposite way, I have still not tried the sex toy that is too strong!'

16

Vibrating ride

Try playing with just the
vibrating buttons first: vary the
speed and just play. If it feels
good, push it in more.

If you're used to a regular vibrator with an on/off switch, it
can be a culture shock to operate a Rabbit with up to three
different buttons, each with multiple control levels! It's
better to try it out on your body first, on a relatively neutral
area, to get used to the feeling. Sex educator Cory Silverberg
says, 'Start with it on your thigh or somewhere else and see
what the vibration feels like, then slowly move it around
your body and find where it feels best. Everybody thinks this
should be self-explanatory, and usually what people do is to

zero in on the most narrowly focused genital region, but we have areas all over our body that respond to vibration in very different ways.'

Once you've worked out which controls and/or speeds feel good, you can head south. Even if you're feeling pretty hot, be liberal with lube. If you're still not turned on, tease your clitoris with the bunny ears.

If you haven't used a vibrator before, then insert just the tip of the shaft, turned off. Does it feel OK? Use more lube if necessary. Experiment with the movement of the ball bearings/pearls which are designed to stimulate this area. Does it feel good? No pressure, just play.

17

The first third

You don't have to push the vibrator all the way in, or even have it buzzing, to experiment with insertion.

Any toy with pearl beads around the shaft is designed to stimulate the nerve endings around the vagina when it's inserted. Most women experience more sensitivity in their clitoris, so to get the most out of using your Rabbit as a penetrative toy it's best to do this in isolation without being tempted by the delicious tickles of the bunny stimulator the first time you try penetration.

Warm up by lightly stimulating yourself, use lube and a couple of fingers to get relaxed enough for penetration. Insert your Rabbit, turned off as if it was just a dildo – there's no need to go too deep. Take it out and switch it on so that the pearl beads/metal balls are whirling. Once again, insert gently and tense your PC muscles around the shaft. Which part of your vagina is most susceptible to friction? Also experiment with the speed. Can you feel more as it increases? It should feel pleasurable and make you crave more vibe action.

Medical intern Will McFee says, 'There aren't many nerve endings the deeper you go into the vagina so the beads stimulate the outside, and the shaft with the movement inside – women may not be able to feel the individual movements, but they get the feeling of being filled, and moving around it gives the impression of it being bigger without having to stretch the opening.'

18

Double stimulation

To use both the vibrating shaft and bunny ears for maximum pleasure, move your hips forwards to shorten the distance.

Depending on the length of your Rabbit and the position of your G-spot, using your vibe as a dual stimulator may take some jiggling! Ideally you'll have chosen a Rabbit that's not too long, that will anatomically be able to pound your G-spot and at the same time fit snugly over your clitoris. Beth Goodale from athenashn.com says, 'The G spot is in a different area for everybody. I'm back there very deep but on some women it's closer to the front of their vaginal wall, so some women have to dig in deep and others don't have to.'

Once you're warmed up, experiment with penetration with your vibe switched off: use your Rabbit as a probe to find your G-spot. Is there an area that feels more pleasurable when you nudge it inside? Don't worry if you haven't located it; line up the bunny ears on your clitoris and go for dual action vibes on a low speed. The internal vibe will feel less intense than the external one, but the combination of a G-spot and clitoral climax could give you a more intense blended orgasm.

Experiment with the speeds, and if the Rabbit feels too long, move your hips forward to shorten the distance inside. You can also lie on one side with your leg raised so you're in a better position to manoeuvre your toy. Experiment and enjoy!

19

The full monty

Once you're enjoying the thrill of both vibrating parts of the Rabbit, switch on the moving pearls to get the Rabbit gyrating inside you for maximum effect.

Although the Rabbit is described as a dual vibrator, in reality it offers a triple whammy. Sex educator Cory Silverberg says, 'The major difference with the Rabbit is that it provides three different kinds of stimulation at once: penetration, clitoral stimulation and the rotation.' Once you've got used to G-spot/clitoral stimulation, experiment with the rotating beads designed to stimulate the sensitive nerve endings just inside your vagina. Some women don't really notice when the rotating sensation is added – they're too distracted elsewhere – but for others this makes the experience the 'full monty'. It's a mechanical way of experimenting with thrusting action and makes it feel more like you're being 'done to'.

In general, the bigger the beads, the more effect you'll feel, with metal ball bearings providing the most intense stimulation, although sexpert Emily Dubberley says, 'Some women prefer the random, swirly action that made the original so memorable, while others prefer it when the balls are in a straight line as they are in the newer models. Every woman is different so experiment to see which you like best.' The specific way in which your Rabbit rotates can also heighten sensitivity; some of the newer models like the iVibe Rabbit Thruster have ball bearings that go up and down rather than round and round to mimic the natural action of a penis. Now do some testing!

20

If you're not feeling turned on

Don't despair if those bunny ears and buttons just don't work for you.

Because sex shops don't offer free testers, choosing a sex toy is very much a process of trial and error. The Rabbit is an exciting and versatile toy for many women, but it may not be the right one for you. Sex educator Cory Silverberg says, 'The drawback of the Rabbit is that you can really only use it when you use it for penetration. It's the kind of toy where the people who like it really like it, but it's not for everyone.' It could be that you need to start with a smaller, simpler toy first and work your way up, or you could reserve it for partner use only.

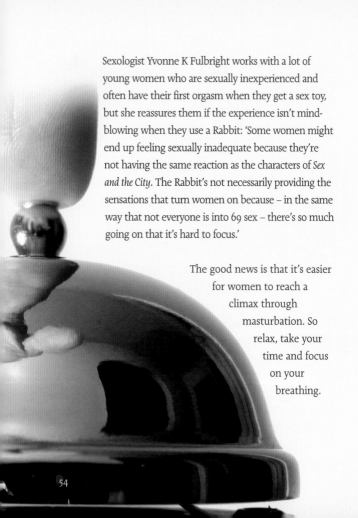

Sexologist Yvonne K Fulbright works with a lot of young women who are sexually inexperienced and often have their first orgasm when they get a sex toy, but she reassures them if the experience isn't mind-blowing when they use a Rabbit: 'Some women might end up feeling sexually inadequate because they're not having the same reaction as the characters of *Sex and the City*. The Rabbit's not necessarily providing the sensations that turn women on because – in the same way that not everyone is into 69 sex – there's so much going on that it's hard to focus.'

The good news is that it's easier for women to reach a climax through masturbation. So relax, take your time and focus on your breathing.

21

Speed tease

If you have a vibrator at one speed on your clitoris for too long it goes numb, so choose a model with variable speeds.

Rabbits come in all shapes and sizes, but their most crucial feature is their vibe action. Some frequencies will get you going more than others, but a model with enhanced features gives you more to play with. Gita Selli, Ann Summers' vibe expert, says, 'If a woman has a vibrator on her clitoris for too long at one speed, the chances are she's going to go numb very quickly, but if it pulsates or has different types of movement, it's more likely to tease her and it means that she can use the clitoral stimulator for a lot longer.'

Ann Summers, for instance, sells five Rabbit models. Some like the Deluxe and Rampant Rabbit have flat speeds, but others pulsate as well. Selli explains, 'With the Platinum Rabbit the clitoral stimulator has seven different vibrations, so you've got three flat beat vibrations which is "zz, zz, zz" and then you have two different pulsations which go from low to high, then you have pulsation and escalation and you also have a sort of escalation where it goes up, up, up, and then it stops and it goes up, up, up, again.'

You can also tease yourself manually by taking the vibe away each time you are on the edge of orgasm. Basically, the longer you can hold out on your clit, the more satisfying it will be when you finally climax.

22

Power burst

Drip lots of lube all over your vulva, put your Rabbit on to its maximum power setting and get ready to play.

Because most Rabbits come with multiple-level settings, you can have fun occasionally blasting yourself with the speed turned up to maximum. This is probably not going to work if you haven't first tantalised yourself by rubbing your vibe everywhere apart from your clitoris. Think of it as vibratory aerobics. Put on a CD with a catchy beat and select a few erogenous zones like your clitoris or outer labia, and combine this with partial vaginal insertion. Simply play a music track and flick your pulsating Rabbit on your chosen hotspots to the beat of the music. Start off using the duller sensation of the shaft's tip, work up to using the more effective bunny ears, and then mix these in combination with dual insertion. Max up the speed, too, as you get going.

Some women say they climax too quickly when they use their toy ordinarily. Rabbit user Nicole Smith says, 'I always go to the highest vibrations very fast.' Chopping and changing vibe action with the help of the music should vary things, distract you and give you a much more satisfying orgasm in the end. This is also a fun game to play with a partner, although do test their sensitivity boundaries carefully first.

23

Your perfect Rabbit

It's not always the biggest and the most expensive model that rocks your boat. Here's how to choose the right one for you.

Finding a sex toy that's perfect for you is all about personal taste. Because Rabbits are so flashy looking, you can get distracted by their extra functions. Avoid automatically buying the deluxe model in the range; this is likely to be longer and thicker, but how this will feel depends on where your G-spot is located. Sex educator Cory Silverberg explains, 'It depends on the Rabbit probe. There are literally hundreds of different Rabbit models, but the original Rabbit Pearl isn't quite as long as other ones. What most people will want is a

shaft that isn't that long – only four or five inches at most. And also that has flexible ears that can move and hug the body.' If the shaft is too long you may have to insert it too deeply for comfort when using the dual vibrations.

At the same time, the appearance and feel of a toy is important. Madeleine Lee says, 'I've never been attracted to a realistic looking vibrator because I don't see it as a surrogate penis.' The trick is to find a toy that is a good fit anatomically, and that you also like. Jill-Evelyn Hellwig from the Fun Factory says, 'Different models don't always give you a different orgasm, it's mainly psychological what you experience. If a vibrator has veins and a penis, you're not going to feel it!'

24

Strong endurance

How to extend the life of your Rabbit vibrator.

Good maintenance not only prolongs the life of your toys, it makes them easier to use too. How you store toys is important. It's better to house them in a cabinet or tool box with separate compartments to keep different materials apart (jelly can dissolve silicone). Always take the batteries out and store them separately. This avoids the possibility of the batteries corroding inside the toy and ensures that they don't get drained down. If the batteries are not working, try using new ones (avoid cheap brands) and rubbing an eraser over the battery tips to improve the connection.

Be careful how you clean your toys and avoid getting the control section wet. Will McFee describes how his partner's overzealousness ruins toys, 'The shaft part is waterproof but the battery compartment is not and she washes it pretty thoroughly and then the water runs down – if you set it on your sink water can wick up into the electronics and break it.' If water does get inside, take the batteries out and use a hairdryer to dry it thoroughly.

Don't run the toy too long – typically they're designed to be used in bursts of about twenty minutes. Avoid bending the shaft too much; this can break if the splint housing the pearls/balls is bent back too far. Finally, it's worth buying a toy case for ease of transport: these look like neutral make-up bags and no one will be any the wiser!

25

Bringing your Rabbit out to play

How to socialise your Rabbit, bring it up in conversation and play with your partner.

Rabbits aren't just for masturbation. Research shows that around half of women use a vibrator during love play with their partner and 4% of male partners borrow the toy for personal use!

The best way to bring up the topic of using sex toys is as a bonus, something naughty that will give you both a buzz. Don't introduce a toy in the middle of foreplay; it's best to talk about it first – perhaps sharing sexual fantasies, or looking at sex toy merchandise.

Sex therapists like Relate specialist Jane Roy often recommend vibrator use for couples. Using toys is now much more acceptable, she says, 'Men seem to be just pleased that their partners have learned to be orgasmic, and happy to use the vibrator if that's what's required.'

Emphasise that he can enjoy the buzz of the vibe too and enjoy watching you pleasure yourself. Sexologist Yvonne K Fulbright says, 'Make it an experience where fun is the only expectation. The more comfortable and in charge she can be, the more confident he can be in return.'

If a phallic-looking vibrator rabbit is too threatening at first, you can start with a purely clitoral vibrator which can also be worn in between you during regular intercourse. (Interestingly, sex researcher Dr Petra Boynton says some men are as threatened by toys that are not phallic-shaped as they are by traditional ones!) If you both feel comfortable with your toy of choice, you're more likely to enjoy it.

Carrie:

"I'm not going to replace a man with some battery-operated device."

Miranda:

"You haven't met 'The Rabbit.'"

The girls from *Sex and the City* talk toys

26

Partner play

Practical exercises to keep you both buzzing.

A good way to initiate Rabbit use is by using it as a simple massager first. It's nicer to smooth lubricant or 'love oil' all over each other for more sensation and to experiment with a throbbing Rabbit in unusual places like the backs of your knees. It's important that you both try out the vibe effects. Sex educator Cory Silverberg says, 'If you've only ever used a vibrator on someone else, you've really only had half the experience – you lack a lot of important information. If a woman comes in and wants a vibrator to use with her partner, I tell them to use it on him first. Most men do like it once they feel it.'

Men will be receptive to the vibrator sensation on the shaft of their penis, nipples and around the anus to stimulate their prostate and testicles. If the vibes make him feel really good, there are also special vibrators for men that are worn around the testicles or base of the penis. If you both feel good and relaxed about vibe play in general, you're more likely to open up and experiment sexually with it together.

A good teasing activity is to rub a throbbing Rabbit on each other's buttocks and tummies before you go on to tickle any sexual parts. Get him to watch you using the bunny ears on yourself so that he can see how you like your clit action and then get him to try it on you. Experiment and, above all, play!

27

Rediscovering intimacy

Use your vibrator to help you rediscover your erotic boundaries.

In a long-term relationship it's all too easy to get stuck in a rut and experience sexual boredom. Using a vibrator allows you to break out of this and to try new things together. Men don't need to feel they are being replaced by a Rabbit; allowing a man to be a part of using it on you will give him new insight into how you tick sexually. Sex toy saleswoman Beth Goodale reckons that about half her customers use their vibrators solo and the other half experiment with partners. She says, 'I tell couples to try everything because they don't know what secrets they might find with it that are intimate for them. I usually tell them to play with it on the balls of the guy and on the clitoris and nipples for the women.'

You can use your Rabbit all over each other, and because a vibe gives much stronger sensations than is possible with a human hand, it's likely to awaken unappreciated erogenous zones. Using a vibrator also helps to build up trust and communication because with a sex toy you can't feel it so well if someone tenses up – so you have to talk to each other about what feels good, and where, and what not to do. Poor communication is often a major cause of sexual problems, so using an exploratory vibe to relearn each other's sexual boundaries can really help. Go for it!

28

How to use the Rabbit on your partner

Saucy tips to get your partner raring to go.

Vibrators can also be stimulating for men – especially if they're having problems getting an erection. If it's taking him too long for comfort to get aroused, you can use a vibrator in conjunction with oral sex to whip him into action. He'll probably feel more sensation on his testicles and at the head of the penis, and using a buzzing vibe on his perineum whilst you're giving him oral sex can also work wonders. Sexpert Emily Dubberley has a special tip for those men who are nervous about vibe play on themselves: 'When

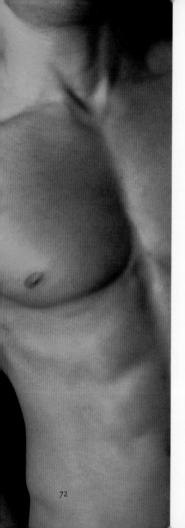

you're doing a blow job, use a vibrator on the outside of your cheek whilst you're doing it because it will make it more intense for the guy. Also holding a standard straight vibrator against the length of the shaft of the penis works well too. That's a good way of stopping a bloke from thinking that sex toys are just for you.'

It might be that a small vibe like the Bunny will work better for partner play than your average Rabbit. Medical intern Will McFee explains, 'If you're having sex with a girl doggy style you can use the vibe on your testicles while you're doing it.' If you encourage your partner to experiment sexually with a vibe, it's much more likely that he'll be enthusiastic about using it on you!

29

Blindfold buzz

Get your lover to blindfold you
and play buzzing Rabbit games
in the dark.

If you're feeling inhibited about letting your lover see you
using a vibe, or allowing him/her to use one on you, then
using blindfolds is a way of releasing you from your
inhibitions. Cutting off one of the senses intensifies the
others and adds to the sense of mystery. It's best to make this
a long-drawn-out process where you take a bath and rub
massage oil all over yourself. Your lover should blindfold you
(use a scarf if you don't have a proper one) and send you to
lie down in a comfortable room. Allow yourself ten minutes
or so just to fantasise and anticipate. Your lover should then

enter with some prepared treats (something like vibes, massage oil, chopped fruits, ice, chocolate sauce). You could engage in dirty talk and then be tantalised by having ice rubbed over your nipples or fruit being softly pressed into your lips. When you're aroused, vibe play starts.

After all the physical sensations on your body, the noise of the humming vibe will now assume more significance. A good trick is for your partner to switch on a number of vibes, hide them in different parts of the room and instruct you to find them. Alternatively, he/she can mix ice and vibe play and see how much teasing you can take, and get you to masturbate wantonly using a vibe. Phew!

30

The warm-up tingle

Use a vibe to wake up your desire only, and then continue with fingers or a partner until you feel ready for more.

You don't have to rely on a vibe for sexual fulfilment. When the German TV show Galileo tested the Fun Factory's products to see what gives you more pleasure, a man or a vibrator, they demonstrated that an orgasm with a partner gives you more intense pleasure than one using a vibrator. However, your Rabbit can be a prop to help boost your libido when your natural desire is flagging, and you can use it just to warm up, or intermittently to pep up your sex drive. Often sex drives between partners are mismatched and a vibe can help redress the balance. Jill-Evelyn Hellwig from the Fun Factory says, 'With the problem of getting turned on between the couple, what we want is that the woman – when she feels she would like to sleep with her partner – to use the stimulation of the vibrator on the clitoris so she can feel turned on in an instant.'

Alternatively, perhaps you feel like playing with yourself but are too lazy to get started. Use the bunny ears to speed up clitoral arousal; it's much faster than any human hand! Once your natural desire is there, you can continue with your fingers. Hands are slower, but you can feel your own juices and responses, and it's fun to alternate between vibe blasts contrasted with the slipperiness of finger play.

31

Panty play

Try using your knickers to keep those vibes close with the minimum of effort.

If you're currently finding your Rabbit's buzz too stimulating or feel too shy to do vibe play fully naked in front of a partner, keeping your panties on keeps your options open. A lot of men fantasise about seeing women in panties, but usually they're thrown off with abandon way too early. Medical intern Will McFee says, 'With a partner you can do panty play. It's sexy to masturbate a girl through her panties and you can do it sneakily in an elevator or in a car without having to take the panties off, and that feels naughty because it is!'

Playing with yourself through the material also enables you to tease yourself. Experiment with different types of material – silk knickers can feel delicious on the skin and make an ideal barrier, allowing you to blast your clitoris with high intensity. If you're feeling lazy and want some help holding your Rabbit in place, panties double up as a vibe holder too. Put your panties down around your ankles and simply raise your legs, hooking the bunny ears through one of the leg holes. You can now have the shaft probing your outer vagina while you bob the bunny ears over your clitoris, or turn it the other way and probe your outer vagina with the gyrating pearls. Panties are a flexible, convenient sex accessory that we wear daily; make use of them!

32

Playing teacher

Your partner can get a better
idea of your erogenous zones
and how you prefer to be
touched by using your Rabbit
on you.

If you are a couple, watching how your female partner uses
the vibrator is a practice exercise in communication. Use
sexual antics with a Rabbit to understand how she likes to be
penetrated and felt. Jill Evelyn-Hellwig from the Fun Factory
says, 'Give the vibrator to him or her to use on you, this way
they can work out what you like. He/she learns much more
about your female sexuality.'

Decide first who will be in control of the vibrator. You could masturbate with it while the other kisses you or performs oral sex. Your partner should look for signs of your arousal like your breathing and the colour and size of your genitals as you get excited. They should pay attention to what kind of foreplay works best and what kind of strokes and hotspots are most effective for you. Once they've watched you pleasure yourself, you can hand control over to them and give instructions on how you want them to use it. The oral communication is crucial. Relate sex therapist Jane Roy knows from experience that talking gets results: 'Couples seem to think that they can work sex out without ever speaking to each other. One of the reasons we get good results is because we improve couples' communication skills vastly.' Pay attention, it's all about showing by doing.

33

Position analysis

Some women want deeper penetration, others find this uncomfortable. Experiment with your Rabbit to find which positions work best for you.

This is not about hanging from the chandeliers. If you're a man, you never really get to assess your partner's reactions when you're having sex, because you're there in situ. Some women don't like full penetration, others are more sensitive just inside, but it's hard to tell during regular sex. This is something you can easily find out using vibrator play. Get her to lie on her side with one leg raised so that it's easier to see and get access to her genitals. Now you can watch as you probe her with a vibe and try different angles and positions. If you want to try something you haven't done, like doggy style or something unusual from the Kama Sutra, you can check out if these are comfortable for her with the help of your flexible friend.

Another option is to use a special G-spot Rabbit model like the Twist & Shake to help locate and pleasure that hidden hotspot. Some men find it difficult to find this using their hands. Jill-Evelyn Hellwig from the Fun Factory says, 'This is why we have G-spot vibrators! The way women want their vagina stimulated is not always the same and the upper vagina can be more sensitive than the lower part, and a vibe makes it easy to stimulate.' Be gentle and patient and you'll learn a few things!

34

Stop faking it

That's right — retrain your partner about how you really get turned on, using your Rabbit to give pointers.

During penetrative sex women are ten times more likely to have problems reaching a climax, but when they masturbate there's a better chance they'll get there. This means a lot of us fake orgasms during partner sex (some men do, too), so once he gets to witness you enjoying your Rabbit, he could be in for a few surprises. It's better, of course, to be able to talk about this as you go along. Relate sex therapist Jane Roy explains how women can end up in this predicament: 'After childbirth a lot of women go back to having sex before they're really mentally or physically ready for it because they feel guilty that their partner's not getting any sex. And they don't enjoy it, so that leads to an expectation that they're not going to – and several years down the line they own up that they're not enjoying it and come to therapy.'

Communication is key, so let your body do the talking so that your partner can see how your body responds sexually. It's harder to describe in words what you want than to demonstrate with a vibe. Try new positions, tantalise erogenous zones you'd normally overlook and experiment. Couples often get into a pattern of having sex, but what you used to like ten years ago may not turn you on now. Discover together what really makes you tick and push the boat out!

35

Double devils

If you're with a partner, try getting them to perform oral sex while they tease you with your Rabbit's vibes.

Adding some vibe action to oral sex can really hot things up. Encourage your partner to take his/her time; it shouldn't be a preamble to the main event. First get them to tease you by licking around the vagina area first. When they dive in, they should experiment with tongue movements like circles, figures of eight and drawing out their name on your clit with their tongue. Straight licks up and down (fence painting) are a no-no. They should use their lips, chin and all parts of their tongue to pleasure you.

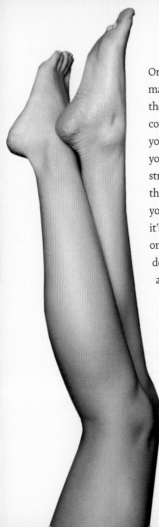

Once you're excited, penetrative play is made easier if you put your legs over their shoulders. They should insert a couple of fingers one at a time and tease you with a buzzing vibe on the outside of your labia rather than putting it in straight away. They can tease you with the bunny on your clit while they lick your vagina underneath. With a Rabbit, it's easier to put a finger cot or condom on the bunny ears and hold it downwards so it buzzes away on your anal area while they tongue your clit. Your partner should avoid making contact with the vibe on their teeth! Periodically, they should switch off the vibe, take it out and just use their mouth. When they reintroduce the toy you'll appreciate it so much more!

86

36

Temperature tease

Varying the temperature of
your Rabbit and your mouth
during oral sex can make for
an extra sensational thrill.

As well as experimenting with speed, vibe frequency and
angles, you can also tease sexually with temperature, and it's
a great technique to use with a partner too. An easy method
is to change the temperature of your vibe. Medical intern
Will McFee says, 'You can put the vibrator in the fridge. Take
the batteries out first and then when it's cold enough simply
put them back in.' If you or your partner like the feeling of
ice down there after being enveloped by a warm tongue, use
small cubes of ice or frozen phallic-shaped objects like Tip

Tops. If whatever you use is too cold, cover it with some cling film or a condom to stop it burning the skin. You could start by teasing with a vibrator and then slowly insert a chilled object before following with sexual intercourse for a whirlwind blast of contrasts.

Ice also works well on the clitoris/testicles and is especially good for giving sensation to women who feel less sensitive in the clitoral area. Another trick is to keep lube in the fridge and to use this lube in conjunction with one that has been warmed in a bowl of warm water for contrast.

Tease and tingle your partner into bliss and get them to try it on you too.

37

What not to do

Avoid the ouch factor by making sure you use your toys correctly.

If you have allergies or a reduced immune system, be picky about toy materials. Generally, silicone is hypoallergenic, but ask the manufacturer for a list of ingredients if you have to avoid certain substances.

Be careful with hygiene, wash toys after use and don't put a clean toy in a sock drawer and use it covered with fluff – it's better to re-wipe it or find a dust-free home for your vibe.

Rabbits are not designed for anal insertion, although some interviewees said they'd successfully done this. Cory Silverberg explains, 'We don't recommend the Rabbit for anal use because it doesn't really work – the movement in the shaft is not that conducive to anal stimulation. It's made more for the vagina.' If you do use it there, or vibrate the bunny ears to tickle the outside of your anus or perineum (the skin between your vagina and anus), don't use the same vibe on your vaginal area – this could spread bacteria. Play safe by using finger cots on the bunny ears or condoms on the shaft and remove before moving to a new area. Similarly, it's easier not to share sex toys, or to put a condom over the toy and take it off before the next one uses it.

Don't fall asleep whilst lying on your toy as you could wake up with a skin burn – and never use mains-powered vibes near water: you don't want to get electrocuted!

HANDLE WITH CARE

38

Confessions of a sex toy tester

Why you shouldn't judge a sex toy by the way it looks.

Emily Dubberley, sexpert and founder of www.cliterati.co.uk, has one of the few jobs in the world where masturbation is part of the job: 'In the last three years I've tested over three hundred sex toys in every single shape and size you can imagine!' From experience she knows you can't judge a toy by the way it looks: 'I've had toys that I've looked at and thought "ew"! The Clit Flipper is a perfect example – I thought it looked rubbish, but it was absolutely amazing.'

She tests toys a couple of times to be fair to them and sometimes it *is* like work, although, 'Quite a lot of the time –

if they're good – even when you start off not in the mood, by the end you're massively horny.' She advises patience and a healthy dose of trial and error to get the best from your vibes. 'Don't expect to fall in love with your first vibrator – I certainly didn't the first time I used one. It might feel a bit weird the first time you try a toy because you have to figure out ways of using it. If you find the vibrations too intense, put your hand underneath it and use it on top of your hand.'

Finally, be wary of your partner's feelings: 'If you go shopping with a partner never, ever go straight to the biggest ones in the shop, it'll make him feel insecure!'

39

Rabbit fever

Some gals become so enamoured with their Rabbit they get kind of addicted. If your Rabbit is becoming too much of a habit, here's what to do.

Stephen Raphael, the writer/producer of the 'mockumentary' *Rabbit Fever,* was prompted to make the film after his friend, Matt Heiman, told him an amazing story: 'He had this girl in his office and she was late for work every day for six weeks until she finally admitted it was because she was using this

Rabbit so much. The idea was so crazy I decided to make a movie about it.' Not that Rabbit users are in danger – all the interviews with vibe-obsessed women were faked. Raphael says, 'I used the Rabbit as a metaphor for all sorts of different things being banned or people being addicted as a way of poking fun at things in society.'

In real life some women allegedly become fixated with their vibrator's regular rhythm – and overuse could make you refrain from using any other way of getting stimulation. Madeleine Lee explains, 'The danger with vibrators is it's just so easy, I got quite hooked to the fact that – without fail – 100% of the time I would come. Whereas with fingers it's more physical and tiring, and the sensation is not the same.'

If you're becoming too fixated by your vibe, remember you don't need to use it every time. You can use it to 'warm up' and then continue with your hand or partner, or use it on alternative erogenous zones.

40

Toys 4 2

If your partner is keen, there are plenty of additional toys to experiment with together.

Most men, despite some initial reservations, enjoy the feel of a vibe once they've tried it, but the Rabbit's size and shape are not ideal if a couple want to incorporate vibe action during sex. Sex educator Cory Silverberg says, 'It's nicer when you have a sex toy that both people can use on each other.'

A good, hands-free vibe that both partners will feel is a vibrating cock-ring; it also has the advantage of helping the man maintain his 'wood'. Another easy one is a clitoral stimulator like the Laya Spot which is flat enough to be in

place on the woman's labia during sex. Double vibes like the Wandering Rabbit have a regular vibe plus a mini one connected by a cord for ease of access so that two can share it. Sometimes the smaller bullet vibes are versatile for couples. Sexpert Emily Dubberley recommends anal bullet vibrators: 'If that's vibrating and the woman's on top then it means that the vibrations travel through the vaginal wall and the fella is getting the feeling of the sexual vibration going on.'

There are also remote-control vibrators for hands-free or partner manipulation, and you can wear them under clothes in public. Finger stimulators like the Fukuoku give anyone magic hands and the Tantra Beam erotic massage system can be worn around his waist to electrify his penis. Happy sex shopping!

"Don't knock masturbation — it's sex with someone I love."

Woody Allen

41

Pregnancy and sex toy use

How keeping in with your Rabbit during pregnancy (and after) can help you to regain your sexual identity.

Sexual activity during pregnancy is rarely discussed, but unless you're at risk of premature labour or placenta previa, sexual pleasure is beneficial. Enthusiastic sex toy user Madeleine Lee used her vibrator throughout her pregnancy: 'In fact, the sensations were far greater when I was pregnant. It's quite amazing, especially in the early weeks, because I could really feel my uterus getting rock hard. Your stomach just becomes your uterus.'

When she was heavily pregnant, sex with her partner changed completely and he became anxious about penetrative sex. During this time vibe play helped her to relax. After a difficult childbirth and multiple stitches, Lee was nervous about resuming sexual activity when the customary six-week healing period was over. 'I thought to myself if I was not going to do it, then I would never do it again. The first couple of times with my partner were quite painful. We made the mistake of not using lubricant – after childbirth, especially if you're breastfeeding, you don't get wet so easily.' At the same time, she stresses how important it is to regain your sexual identity: 'If you don't use it, you lose it, it's like everything else. You need to feel sexy again and you might not feel sexy because your boobs are enormous or because you haven't lost the weight. I think it helped me to use a vibrator – it made me me again.'

42

Multiple buzz

Once you've had one orgasm, try switching the vibrating pulses to a lower setting and start teasing your outer lips again.

One of the advantages of vibrators is that it's so much easier for a woman to get aroused and to climax using one. In addition, women tend to be more multi-orgasmic than men because once they've got there it takes them less time to hit the plateau stage again. Although not all women find it easy, some can have a second orgasm at the touch of a button. Nicole Smith reckons it takes her under five minutes to climax the second time: 'When I'm by myself I turn down the power for just a few minutes and leave the vibrator inserted where it is, then take it out and use it on the clitoris for a bit and it works again!'

You might need to wait longer or keep the sexual tension focused on a secondary erogenous zone – like your nipples – that's not so sensitive. The great thing is that vibes work well with partners, especially if your sex drives are mismatched. Danish sexologist Helle Koldsø says, 'Obviously if she's had the first orgasm with the help of a vibrator, it's going to be easier for her to get a second and third orgasm afterwards with her partner. Often women only need one orgasm to have more and it's such an easy thing to use the vibrator to let her start before him, with him doing it to her.'

43

G it up!

Once you've comfortably inserted your Rabbit, try switching on the gyrating part to hunt for your G-spot.

The traditional vibrator was straight, but this doesn't fit to the natural shape of your vagina or do much for your G-spot, whereas the Rabbit is specifically designed for dual stimulation. Gita Selli, Ann Summers' vibe expert, says, 'The reason why the Rabbit is so popular is because it gives you a blended orgasm where the woman has two orgasms in one go – there's G-spot as well as clitoral stimulation.'

Some Rabbits are specially curved, like the Fun Factory's Twist & Shake, to help you find that elusive spot. A toy might help you because it gives concentrated pressure on the area you are trying to nudge. Sometimes the probe of a vibe helps you get there, but this could also prove distracting, so insert your Rabbit with and without vibes.

Sex retailer Beth Goodale says, 'A lot of women aged forty to sixty are just finding out about the G-spot now because in their era they didn't talk about such things. And they're realising they like both the clit and G-spot stimulation and they like it a lot!' Another handy thing about your vibe is that it helps your partner to feel more comfortable about helping you locate the spot. Jill Evelyn-Hellwig from the Fun Factory says, 'Some men feel uncomfortable inserting fingers into the vagina to feel for the G-spot so they can use a special G-spot vibrator instead.'

44

Masturbation habits

Sexperts talk about breaking away from your old ways of finding bliss.

If you're over thirty, then it's likely you didn't grow up having easy access to vibrators. Sex stores used to be murky dens of iniquity frequented by men, and so your formative experiences where you learned masturbation techniques will probably have involved a lot of diddling. Sex retailer Beth Goodale says, 'A lot of people from that generation usually use their hands. They stay a little further away from vibrators and usually go for items with more clitoral stimulation.'

Sexologist Helle Koldsø admits she also got used to masturbating in a certain way, but after a couple of years

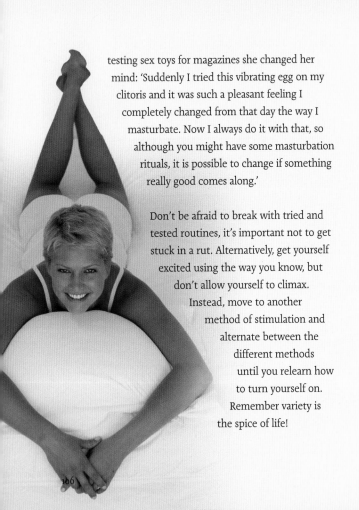

testing sex toys for magazines she changed her mind: 'Suddenly I tried this vibrating egg on my clitoris and it was such a pleasant feeling I completely changed from that day the way I masturbate. Now I always do it with that, so although you might have some masturbation rituals, it is possible to change if something really good comes along.'

Don't be afraid to break with tried and tested routines, it's important not to get stuck in a rut. Alternatively, get yourself excited using the way you know, but don't allow yourself to climax. Instead, move to another method of stimulation and alternate between the different methods until you relearn how to turn yourself on. Remember variety is the spice of life!

45

Gaining sexual confidence

Believe in yourself.

Hopefully your Rabbit has helped you to explore your sexuality, and maybe its vibe has finally tipped you over the edge into having your first orgasm or multiple climax. However, it's important to remember that it's just a tool – your biggest sex organ is actually your brain. Sex educator Cory Silverberg says, 'Sex toys are not necessarily the answer to sexual problems. They are not a magic bullet, they can be wonderful and amazing, but sometimes I worry that sex toys will become the next thing that people just have to do.'

If your vibe has helped you to break down sexual barriers and lose some inhibitions – great, but also work on building up your self-esteem. Sex researcher Dr Petra Boynton says,

'People have problems with confidence, communication and body image before they are encouraged to see lack of desire as a medicalised female sexual dysfunction.'

Learning new techniques and getting sexual satisfaction often does boost your confidence, but it's no good unless deep down you feel comfortable with who you are. Relate sex therapist Jane Roy thinks better sex education from schools and assurance from parents could help women to feel more like they own their own body: 'Being able to take pleasure from your own body would help enormously. It's surprising how many people don't know about the clitoris, for example; it's still not included in basic school sex education which is about reproduction.' It's simple – if you love yourself, your body will respond in kind.

46

Shaven ravers

Try experimenting with hair removal on your most sensitive bits to maximise Rabbit action.

Shaving your pubic hair allows you to feel more sensation on your bare skin – be it a tongue, finger or buzzing vibe. In addition, your partner also gets to see more of the vibe in action when you play. If you don't want to go the whole hog, consider removing the hair around the clitoral hood or on your outer lips – these are where you'll feel the difference most. One of the pluses is that you'll be more receptive to temperature and touch – even your panties will feel different! But take care, sexpert Emily Dubberley recommends: 'One thing is universally use lube if you're going to be shaved, because otherwise you might chafe the skin.'

When you begin Rabbit play on your new coif, start with a lower speed than usual. Drizzle yourself with lube and draw circles around the outside of your labia. Explore every inch of your new bare skin. You might find that areas that you previously overlooked, like your outer lips, now feel more sexual. Try tricks like tantalising just one side of your vagina; when you get to the other side it will be prickling in anticipation. You can also try lying on top of your vibe and feeling the whole thing pulsing underneath you. Aim to wake up the whole of your vaginal area and tickle yourself with your Rabbit into a satisfying climax.

47

The doggy – Rabbit style

Most people masturbate with a Rabbit vibrator lying on their back, but other positions offer a different sensation.

Rabbit vibrators are designed for vaginal and clitoral stimulation, but you can also use them for light external stimulation of the anal area. Sex toy retailer Beth Goodale, who works for www.athenashn.com, talks about her favourite position to use her Rabbit: 'I usually do doggy style because that way it's coming in from a different area and if women want a little bit of anal stimulation instead of clitoral stimulation, you can twist the Rabbit around so that the ears are hitting up against your anus. Plus the way the vibrator is being inserted in you from behind also has a different sensation; it's easier to hit your G-spot from behind.'

This position is ideal for partner experimentation. And you can take things one step further by experimenting with accessories like strategically placed pillows or a love swing that hangs from the ceiling – giving you access to a wider range of body positioning.

The bunny ears of the anal stimulator are designed to stimulate the nerve endings around the anus and can be used internally. Don't use the shaft for anal insertion though, as the sphincter muscles are much stronger than vaginal ones and could damage your toy. As long as you take care not to use the same part of the toy to rub against both your anal and vaginal area, the 'doggy' is an exciting alternative position for solo or partner play.

48

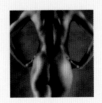

Love muscle

Strengthening your PC muscles helps to increase your pleasure. Here are some simple techniques for using your Rabbit to exercise your love muscles.

The best way to achieve better orgasms is to strengthen and tighten your pelvic floor muscles, and you can use your Rabbit as a sex tool to help you locate and work these out. You could start by inserting a finger and then clenching until you can feel it. Ensure you are well lubricated and then insert your Rabbit turned off (as if it was a dildo). Clench around the Rabbit, release and repeat up to ten times. Have a rest and try again. Research suggests that using some form of resistance helps your muscles to develop three times faster.

Sexologist Yvonne K Fulbright explains, 'Some women prefer using a sex toy in strengthening their PC muscle. Being able to grip a toy, or noticing a difference in vaginal muscle grip around a vibrator, like the Rabbit, can not only help you to gauge the effectiveness of your pelvic floor muscles during exercises, but any improvement in strength as well.'

Advanced techniques include lying in different positions like on your side, on your stomach and on all fours; you can also try to clench your muscles to push your vibe completely out. Get the pearl beads whirling and try resisting against that added pressure as well. As an added bonus, if you have a male partner, try clenching on your boyfriend's penis as well.

49

Travelling with your Rabbit

How to pack your Rabbit discreetly and get it through customs.

Don't be embarrassed to travel with sex toys – they could be just the thing to pep up a fortnight on the beach – but here are some tips to make the process hassle-free.

Where possible, pack toys into luggage that will be checked in. A BAA representative from London Heathrow explains, 'All luggage that goes on an aircraft is screened for security purposes. While we are mainly looking for things that could be a security threat, it is true that other items, including electronic devices, are readily identifiable. If somebody felt that they might be embarrassed by what they were carrying in their hand luggage, an alternative is to pack the item in their suitcase. It will still get X-rayed but the bag won't be readily associated with a person unless there is a security issue.'

Always take the batteries out before packing. If you travel with the batteries intact, there's more of a chance your toy will receive special security screening, and the toy could turn itself on and cause a security alert. This happened to traveller Renee Koutsouradis who later sued Delta Airlines for the way they handled the incident!

It's easiest to avoid Rabbits that contain metal balls. Ensure your toys are clean, wrap them in a cloth or buy a special travel bag for ease of mobility. Also check that sex toys are not prohibited in the country you're travelling to; certain Middle Eastern countries will confiscate them.

50

Down the slippery slope

Using the right lubricant for your toy and other smeary accessories to keep you happy.

Lubricants are great for general love play (even a simple hand job is friendlier with a glob of lube). However, it's important to use a compatible lube for your toy. Silicone lube is slick, but can damage silicone sex toys. Oil-based lube is great, but harder for the vagina to flush out afterwards and can damage latex condoms. The most common lube is a water-based one; it's compatible with all toys/condoms, but tends to dry up faster and often contains glycerine which can cause thrush if women are susceptible to it.

There are a lot of lubes out there, so experiment to find out what consistency/type suits you. Sexologist Yvonne K Fulbright says, 'Some products in the USA have done well because they've had the backing of the medical community, for example K-Y jelly. A lot of people don't know they have other options.' It's easy to buy some lube samplers (available from most online sex stores) and test them out. If you have sensitive skin generally, masturbate in the lube with your fingers first to check your reaction before going mad with your Rabbit.

There are also massage oils and rub-on creams for the clitoris that have a tingle effect. These can be great – or too intense. An easy test for sensitivity: if your partner goes down on you after brushing their teeth, how do you react to the minty residue? Play hard, but keep things smooth.

51

Adapting Rabbit play around disabilities

Cory Silverberg on how folks with fatigue or disabilities can adapt and choose toys for ease of use.

Sex toys are often badly designed for people with disabilities because manufacturers often design toys based on how they look rather than how they feel. Cory Silverberg, co-author of *The Ultimate Guide to Sex and Disability,* says, 'It's crucial that everyone selecting a sex toy actually gets the chance to feel the toy before they purchase, especially those with disabilities for whom the ease of using a switch is essential.

For some it's about finding a light vibrator – it might be something like the Fukuoku that fits on the finger, but for others it's about finding a large, heavy vibrator they could lie beside.'

Other options include remote-controlled toys that might be easier to operate, or a vibrator attached to a long wand like the Flex-O-Pleaser which allows people with reduced mobility to reach their genitals. Silverberg also offers tips on adapting sex toys using items like foam and tape on www.comeasyouare.com.

Vibrators are particularly effective for people with reduced sensation. Silverberg says, 'Vibrators provide intense stimulation that we can't provide ourselves, regardless of disability – no human being works as fast as a vibrator.' Ensure you are able to turn the vibrator off, though, and be wary of overheating.

Your sexual well-being helps to boost your general health, so don't be afraid to ask for help from doctors, and query shops about issues like the weight and size of toys and what they're made out of.

52

The future of vibrators

As well as better toys, we'll need more access to information in order to get the best out of the buzz.

In the future, sex toy manufacturers will probably move towards self-regulation to give customers more assurance. They'll list the product contents and supply more detailed product literature. Companies like the Fun Factory already use only medical grade silicone, and Ann Summers is one of the few sex toy retailers to have their own quality assurance department to monitor suppliers – and aligns itself to the same safety standards as children's products that may be mouthed.

Sex toys are likely to be more accessible; Durex is expanding into vibrators to try to open up the market. However, this will only work if it's combined with more education on how to use products. Juliane Bessner from the Fun Factory thinks they would sell millions of Laya Spot clitoral vibes if women knew what to do with them: 'Often the people who buy our products don't have the fantasy or imagination to use them.'

It seems people are reluctant to talk about what they actually do with their Rabbits. Sex researcher Dr Petra Boynton says, 'The Rabbit has become a cultural icon and women's magazines mention it so much because everybody knows what that product is without having to describe what it does. They don't really want to talk about what sex toys do, or where they go.' Hopefully things will start to change. For the future to be buzzing, we need to be more open and relaxed about our sexuality. Enjoy!

Interviewees...

Juliane Bessner is a PR representative for the innovative sex toy manufacturer Fun Factory (Germany), see www.funfactory.de.

Dr Petra Boynton has a PhD in Applied Human Psychology and lectures in health services research. She is the sex editor of www.menshealth.co.uk and the author of *The Research Companion: A Practical Guide for the Social and Health Sciences*. She has written on sexuality for the *New Scientist*, the *Guardian* and numerous publications. See www.drpetra.co.uk.

Emily Dubberley is a leading sexpert and author of numerous books including *Brief Encounters: The Women's Guide to Casual Sex*, *Sex Play* and *Sex for Busy People*. She contributes to many magazines and radio shows including *Cosmopolitan*, www.ivillage.co.uk, London Live and *Kerrang!* See www.cliterati.co.uk and www.dubberly.com.

Yvonne K Fulbright is an Icelandic sexologist currently completing a PhD in International Community Health in the USA. She is the author of *Touch Me Here: A Hands-On Guide to Your Orgasmic Hot Spots* and *The Hot Guide to Safer Sex*.

Beth Goodale is a US-based sex toy saleswoman for athenashn.com.

Jill-Evelyn Hellwig is a sales representative for the Fun Factory and travels internationally talking to female-friendly sex stores. See www.funfactory.de.

Helle Koldsø is a Danish sexologist and she regularly tests sex toys for magazines, see www.houseofillusion.dk. She was casting director for the Danish erotic film, *All About Anna* (2005).

Juli-Ann Ledger is a saleswoman who works from home in England and is an enthusiastic Rabbit user.

*Madeleine Lee is an international data manager for an online distributor and is an enthusiastic Rabbit user.

*Will McFee is a US medical intern based in Germany and knows a thing or two about vibrators.

Stephen Raphael is the writer/producer of the 'mockumentary' *Rabbit Fever* (2006).

Jane Roy is the training coordinator for Relate, the UK's largest provider of relationship counselling and sex therapy. See www.relate.org.uk.

Gita Selli, Ann Summers' vibe expert, is responsible for corporate-wide staff training for a company that invented the idea of female-friendly sex shops and made these accessible in the UK. See www.annsummers.com.

Cory Silverberg is a sex educator and has a Masters degree in Counselling Psychology. He is the co-author of *The Ultimate Guide to Disability* and a founding member of the Toronto-based sex shop Come As You Are: www.comeasyouare.com. He also contributes to http://sexuality.about.com.

*Nicole Smith is an event management planner and enthusiastic Rabbit user. She is based in Germany.

* denotes use of pseudonym.

brilliant ideas

The user's guide to the Rabbit is published by Infinite Ideas, publishers of the acclaimed **52 Brilliant Ideas** series. There are over 45 titles published in the series over subject areas as diverse as Health & relationships; Sports, hobbies & games; Lifestyle & leisure and Careers, Finance & personal development. To find out more visit **www.infideas.com**, or e-mail **info@infideas.com**.

Brilliant Sizzling Sex Series Book offer

Exclusive to readers of *The user's guide to the Rabbit* – get £2 off the next book in our sexy new series

If Marcelle Perks has tempted you and your Rabbit into action why not try the next book in this series for more inspiring ideas.

Erotic fantasies provides 52 tips and techniques sure to get your libido racing and transform your sexual appetite. This book will ensure that your trip to fantasy island is one to remember. Revealing the top 10 sexual surprises, the art of dirty dancing, electrifying role plays and luscious locations to give them a whirl, *Erotic fantasies* will stimulate your mind and a few other areas too!

To get your copy of *Erotic fantasies* (available August 2006) at an exclusive discounted price of £4.99 with free p&p (usual price £6.99) simply fill in the form below, cut out or photocopy and send to Infinite Ideas, 36 St Giles, Oxford OX1 3LD along with a cheque for £4.99.*

Alternatively email **orders@infideas.com** providing your full name and email address and quoting promotional code **'Fantasies52'**. We will email you details of how to claim your exclusive discount and purchase the book* safely and securely through our website, www.infideas.com.

*Please note that no payment will be taken until your purchase has been dispatched.

--✂------

Name:...

Delivery address:..

 ....

 ....

 ....

Email:...

Telephone: ....

Offer code: Fantasies52

LoveH♥NEY®.co.uk
Sexy and Secure Adult Shopping

LoveHoney and Infinite Ideas have teamed up to offer readers of *The user's guide to the Rabbit* this FREE gift!

You're holding the definitive guide to getting the most out of your Rabbit vibrator. So why not make sure you own the world's most popular and ultimate sex toy? When you buy the **Tracey Cox Supersex Rabbit Vibe** at LoveHoney you'll get a Tracey Cox Supersex Silicone Luxury Lube worth £7.99, absolutely **FREE**.

The Sex Inspectors presenter Tracey Cox is one of the world's foremost writers on sex, body language and relationships. Her books *Supersex* and *Hot Sex* are international bestsellers and she has sold over a million books worldwide. Tracey has teamed up with LoveHoney to produce a Rabbit that's easier to use, more powerful, and best of all – quieter than any other Rabbit on the market!

〉〉〉〉〉

LOVEH♥NEY®.co.uk
Sexy and Secure Adult Shopping

Exclusively available at LoveHoney, the **Tracey Cox Supersex Rabbit Vibe** is ultra-quiet, ultra-powerful, and designed to give you intense, immense orgasms with little or no effort. And with your **FREE Supersex Silicone Lube** it's the ultimate in solo satisfaction!

HOW TO GET YOUR FREE TUBE OF LUBE

To get your free **Luxury Lube,** which usually retails at £7.99, simply visit **www.lovehoney.co.uk/rabbitguide** When you order your **Supersex Rabbit Vibe** and **Supersex Luxury Lube** here, the price of the lube will automatically be removed at the checkout.

Offer available while stocks last. Offer only available to readers of *The user's guide to the Rabbit.*